Creating Speeches That Work

How To Create A Speech That Will Make Your Message Be Remembered Forever!

"Practical, proven techniques that will help you to make your next speech a success"

Dr. Jim Anderson

Published by:
Blue Elephant Consulting
Tampa, Florida

Printed in the United States of America

Library of Congress Control Number: 2017932138

ISBN-13: 978-1542756242
ISBN-10: 1542756243

Warning – Disclaimer

The purpose of this book is to educate and entertain. This book does not promise or guarantee that anyone following the ideas, tips, suggestions, techniques or strategies will be hired. It is the discretion of employers if you will or will not be hired. The author, publisher and distributor(s) shall have neither liability nor responsibility to anyone with respect to any loss or damage caused, or alleged to be caused, directly or indirectly by the information contained in this book.

Other Books By
The Author

Product Management

- Managing Your Product Manager Career: How Product Managers Can Find And Succeed In The Right Job

- How Product Managers Can Sell More Of Their Product: Tips & Techniques For Product Managers To Better Understand How To Sell Their Product

Public Speaking

- How To Organize A Speech In Order To Make Your Point: How to put together a speech that will capture and hold your audience's attention

- Changing How You Speak To Overcome Your Fear Of Speaking: Change techniques that will transform a speech into a memorable event

CIO Skills

- New IT Technology Issues Facing CIOs: How CIOs Can Stay On Top Of The Changes In The Technology That Powers The Company

- Keeping The Barbarians Out: How CIOs Can Secure Their Department and Company: Tips And Techniques For CIOs To Use In Order To Secure Both Their IT Department And Their Company

IT Manager Skills

- How IT Managers Can Use New Technology To Meet Today's IT Challenges: Technologies That IT Managers Can Use In Order to Make Their Teams More Productive

- How To Build High Performance IT Teams: Tips And Techniques That IT Managers Can Use In Order To Develop Productive Teams

Negotiating

- Getting What You Want In A Negotiation By Learning How To Signal: How To Develop The Skill Of Effective Signaling In A Negotiation In Order To Get The Best Possible Outcome

- Exploring How To Get The Deal That You Want In A Negotiation: How To Develop The Skill Of Exploring What Is Possible In A Negotiation In Order To Reach The Best Possible Deal

Miscellaneous

- How To Heal A Broken Leg – Fast!: Understanding how to deal with a broken leg in order to start walking again quickly

- How Software Defined Networking (SDN) Is Going To Change Your World Forever: The Revolution In Network Design And How It Affects

- **Note**: See a complete list of books by Dr. Jim Anderson at the back of this book.

Acknowledgements

Any book like this one is the result of years of real-world work experience. In my over 25 years of working for 7 different firms, I have met countless fantastic people and I've been mentored by some truly exceptional ones. Although I've probably forgotten some of the people who made me the person that I am today, here is my attempt to finally give them the recognition that they so truly deserve:

- Thomas P. Anderson
- Art Puett
- Bobbi Marshall
- Bob Boggs

Dr. Jim Anderson

6

This book is dedicated to my wife Lori. None of this would have been possible without her love and support.

Thanks for the best years of my life (so far)...!

Speaking.   Negotiating.   Managing.   Marketing.

Table Of Contents

Creating A Speech That Works

Let's face it, creating a speech is hard work. However, as long as we are going to go to the effort of creating a speech, it sure seems like we should do a good job of it. Now the difficult part comes: just exactly how does one go about creating a speech that works?

We need to keep in mind the fact that we are never creating a generic speech. Instead, we're creating a specific speech for a specific audience. What this means is that we need to customize our speech to our audience. Our ultimate goal is to be able to create a speech that is so good that we are able to cast a spell over our audience.

We want our audience to listen to what we have to say. This means that we need to find ways to get them to view us as being the experts on what we are talking about. If we want them to remember what we've told them, then we need to find ways to make them laugh during our speech. This is no easy thing to accomplish.

In our hopes of getting our audience to listen to us, we all struggle with the same sets of questions. Will they believe us? This comes down to the age old question of if an audience will believe what you are telling them because of who you are or because of how you tell them. If you have not had time to prepare a formal speech, then you had better be good at thinking on your feet!

The only tool that we have to work with when we are giving a speech is words. What words we use and how we put them together can allow us to create powerful speeches that can change how people think. When we are creating these speeches we need to keep in mind the fact that the best speeches often have a great deal of us in them.

For more information on what it takes to be a great public speaker, check out my blog, The Accidental Communicator, at:

www.TheAccidentalCommunicator.com

Good luck!

- Dr. Jim Anderson

About The Author

I must confess that I never set out to be a public speaker. When I went to school, I studied Computer Science and thought that I'd get a nice job programming and that would be that. Well, at least part of that plan worked out!

My first job was working for Boeing on their F/A-18 fighter jet program. I spent my days programming fighter jet software in assembly language and I loved it. The U.S. government decided to save some money and went looking for other countries to sell this plane to. This put me into an unfamiliar role: I started to meet with foreign military officials and I ended up having to give speeches in order to explain what my product did.

Time moved on and so did I. I found myself working for Siemens, the big German telecommunications company. They were making phone switches and selling them to the seven U.S. phone companies. The problem was that the switches were too complicated. Customers couldn't tell the difference between one complicated phone switch from another complicated phone switch. Once again I found myself standing in front of the room giving speeches in order to explain what these complicated machines did and why ours were better than anyone else's.

I've spent over 25 years working as a product manager for both big companies and startups. This has given me an opportunity to do many, many presentations for customers, at conferences, and everywhere in-between.

I now live in Tampa Florida where I spend my time managing my consulting business, Blue Elephant Consulting, teaching college courses at the University of South Florida, and traveling to work with companies like yours to share the knowledge that I have about how to create and deliver powerful and effective speeches.

I'm always available to answer questions and I can be reached at:

Dr. Jim Anderson
Blue Elephant Consulting
Email: jim@BlueElephantConsulting.com
Facebook: http://goo.gl/1TVoK
Web: **www.BlueElephantConsulting.com**

"Unforgettable communication skills that will set your ideas free..."

Create Speeches That Motivate Your Audiences And Get Your Message Heard!

Dr. Jim Anderson is available to provide training and coaching on the topics that are the most important to people who have to speak in public: how can I create a speech that people want to hear and how can I deliver in a way that will allow me to connect with my audience and get my point across to them?

Dr. Anderson believes that in order to both learn and remember what he says, speakers need to laugh. Each one of his speeches is full of fun and humor so that what he says "sticks" with everyone.

Dr. Anderson's Public Speaking Training Includes:

1. How to plan your next speech: pick your purpose and understand your audience.
2. What's the best way to get PowerPoint and Keynote to work with you, not against you?
3. What do you need to do when you are presenting in order to truly connect with your audience?

Dr. Jim Anderson presents over 100 speeches per year. To invite Dr. Anderson to speak at your event, contact him at:

Phone: 813-418-6970 or
Email: jim@BlueElephantConsulting.com

Blue
Elephant
Consulting
Speaking   Negotiating   Managing   Marketing

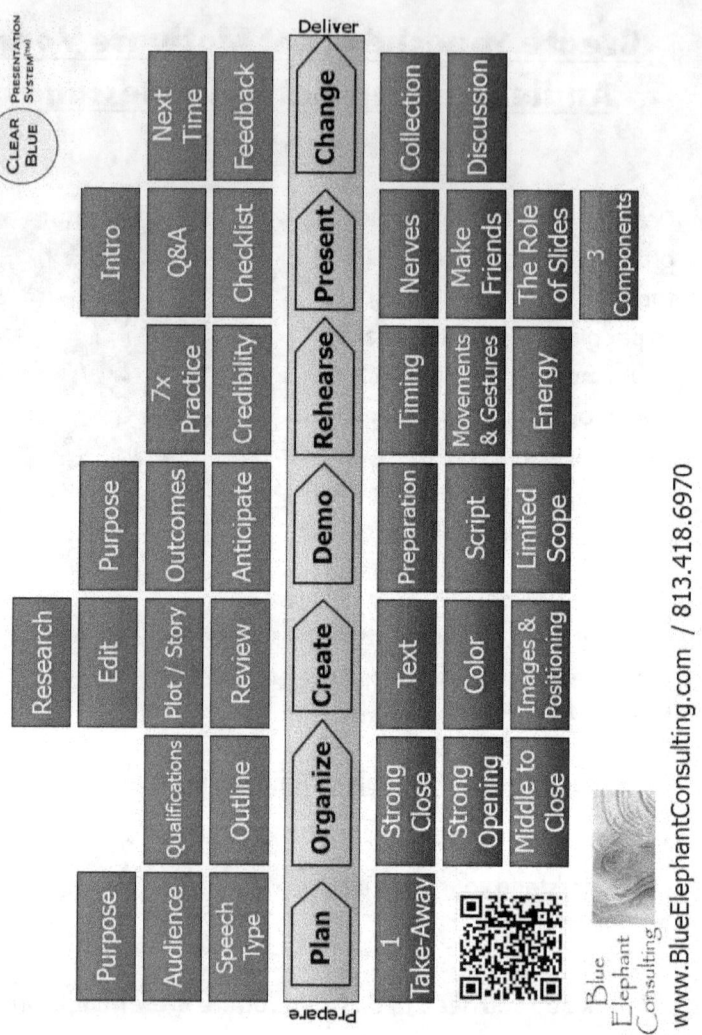

Blue Elephant Consulting has created the **Clear Blue™** presentation system for creating and delivering powerful and memorable presentations. The contents of this book are based on lessons learned during the development of the Clear Blue system. Contact Blue Elephant Consulting to learn more about the Clear Blue presentation system.

Chapter 1

Size Matters – Shaping Your Speech To Match Your Audience

Chapter 1: Size Matters – Shaping Your Speech To Match Your Audience

Have you ever heard the expression "**one size fits all**"? I'm not sure what this phrase was invented to describe, but I can tell you that it sure wasn't public speaking. Something that too many public speakers don't realize is that you need to create different speeches for different size audiences. There is **no such thing** as the one-size-fits-all speech.

Types Of Audiences

One of the first questions that has to be answered is just **how many** different size audiences are there out there? Cliff Suttle has taken a look at this and he believes that there are four different common audience sizes:

- **Conversation Size**: an audience of up to 10 people.

- **Speech Size**: an audience of 10-40 people.

- **Performance Size**: an audience of 40-100 people.

- **Show Size**: an audience of 100 or more people

The reason that the size of your audience matters is because you need to **tune your speech** to meet the needs of that size audience. Just as a clown at a birthday party does different things to entertain its audience from what a comedian at a nightclub does, so too does a public speaker need to make changes to suit the size of his/her audience.

How To Match Your Speech To Your Audience's Size

Once you know how large of an audience you'll be talking to, you can adjust your speech to best match the needs of that audience. You'll have to take a **different approach** for each type of audience:

- **Conversation Size**: the key to satisfying this type of audience is to NOT deliver a formal speech. Instead what you want do is to have an intimate conversation with them. You'll need to be able to be flexible in order to adjust your speech to meet the changing moods of your audience.

- **Speech Size**: the audience size is still small enough that you are going to be able to use a conversational tone, but you are going to have prepare and deliver a formal speech. Eye contact becomes very important and you need to make hand gestures in order to include everyone in your speech.

- **Performance Size**: for this type of speech, taking the time to memorize your speech can be a big help because it will free you up to focus on HOW you say it. You are going to have to speed up the eye contact and not spend too much time looking at any one person. If you make your audience laugh, be sure to give the entire audience time to laugh before you start speaking again.

- **Show Size**: One of the most important points about speaking to a large audience has nothing to do with your words – it's all about self-confidence. Being confidant and taking and owning the stage are critical parts of winning a large audience over to your side.

There will no longer be an opportunity to make eye contact with individuals in the audience, instead you'll have to look at sections of the audience in such a way that they all feel as though you are looking at them individually. Your use of vocal variety becomes critical to keeping your audience engaged in your speech.

Final Thoughts

All too often when we are asked to give a speech we will spend all of our time thinking about the speech and not spend any time **thinking about the audience**. All audiences are not created the same. We need to **tailor** our speeches to meet the needs of the size audience that we are addressing.

When preparing a speech always **plan for the big show**. Then spend some extra time scaling it down to match your audience. This way you'll have a backup plan if more people happen to show up.

Learn to do this well and you'll be able to intimately connect with your audience and make a **lasting impact** in their lives.

Chapter 2

Speechwriting Magic: 3 Ways To Cast A Spell Over Your Audience

Chapter 2: Speechwriting Magic: 3 Ways To Cast A Spell Over Your Audience

When you deliver a speech you stand up straight, you speak clearly, and you have fantastic eye contact. What more could anyone ask for? How about a speech that is **both memorable and magical...**

Do Your Homework

If you want to create a speech that will do **the two most difficult things that any speaker can attempt, inspire and motivate your audience**, then you're going to need to write a killer speech. That speech is only going to be as good as what you are able to put into it. This means that you've got some homework to do.

If you wait until when you are sitting down to create your next speech to start to collect the information that you are going to need to make a great speech, then **it may already be too late**. The really good speechwriters are always collecting information. They read everything that they can get their hands on and those items that catch their attention get filed away somewhere they can find it when they eventually need it.

Your ultimate goal needs to have **more information that you've collected for your speech than you could possibly use**. This will allow you to sort through it all and pick out only the best bits to use.

Magic Speeches Start One Word At A Time

What's interesting about speech writing is that all too often **we are our own worst enemies**. We all know what a great speech sounds like and as we are creating a speech we quickly realize that our first draft basically sounds pretty lousy. If you aren't careful, you can get caught in an almost endless loop of editing in which you try to get a sentence perfect before you write the next one.

Don't do this. Instead **just let the words flow out of you** as you create your first pass of the speech. One way to make sure that your speech is able to grab your audience's attention and holds it is to identify 6 or so main points that will grab attention and which have a good story associated with them.

As you practice your speech, what you are going to be listening for is the **"rhythm"** that your speech has: it has a lot to do with the pace of the speech and how it all links together.

It's All About The Ears

I can't tell you how much time I've spent in the past working on **getting my Power Point slides just perfect**. It turns out that this is not what I should have been doing. Your audience really isn't going to remember what your slides looked like after your speech is over. Instead, it's your words that will stay with them if you choose them correctly.

If you take the time to make sure that your words are used to **draw a sequence of mental pictures in your audience's heads** then you will have found a way to leave a lasting impression. An important note here is that we write differently than we speak – we use more slang and contractions when we are speaking. If you write your speech out and then read it as you wrote it, it's not going to come across as a natural way of speaking.

What All Of This Means For You

Finding a way to cast **a magical spell** over your audience is what every speaker wants to find a way to do. Creating a great speech is one way to make this happen.

The way to make happen is to **get into your audience's head** while you are writing your next speech. Once you do this you'll understand that your audience doesn't really want to find out just how smart you are (what can they do with that?), but rather what they really want is to know what they can do with the information that you share with them during your speech...

Chapter 3

The Secret To Becoming An Expert In Anything

Chapter 3: The Secret To Becoming An Expert In Anything

If you forget all of the advice that you've ever been given about speaking, then please at least remember this: **audiences come to hear experts speak**. No matter how badly you stutter, lose your place, don't make eye contact, etc. an audience will always forgive a presenter whom they believe is an expert in what he/she is talking about.

What Is An Expert?

Great I hear you saying, but just what is an expert? It turns out that this is a pretty simple question to answer: an expert is someone who **knows more about a topic than the audience does**. It really is that simple.

It's not easy to become an expert; however, it is possible. The key to success is to transform yourself into a **non-stop learning machine** that is never satisfied with what you already know.

How Can You Become An Expert?

Shawn Doyle is a speaker who has looked into the whole "become an expert" thing and he's found the secret. He says that the key is to **get motivated and stay motivated**.

Perhaps you thought that learning stopped when you got out of school? Sadly some people do; however, with any luck they are out there sitting in your audience. It's really not that hard to acquire additional knowledge if you know the secret of how to do it. At the heart of knowledge is books and it turns out that, just like your mom told you all those years ago, **the more you read, the smarter you'll be.**

Are you groaning yet? Complaining that you read magazines (while you are standing in line waiting to check out at the supermarket) but you haven't read a book in years? It turns out that the time that you spent in school was just a brief part of your overall life (hopefully) and **continuing to learn** is something that you need to keep doing for your entire life if you want people to show up and listen to you.

Steps To Becoming An Expert

Another name for an expert is "**learner**". If you want to find a way to work learning into your already busy schedule, then you are going to have find out how to find the knowledge that you need in order to wow your audiences. The good news is that I'm going to tell you how to do this.

Learners read books. They might also watch TV, they might surf the web, they might do a lot of things, but most importantly they read books. Not only do they read books, they have a plan for what books they are going to read. They create a monthly list of the books that they are going to read. They add books to their list by asking other people that they know and respect what books they are reading.

If you are going to become a learner in order to become an expert, then you are going to have to start doing **more reading** than you are doing today. Here are some suggestions for how you can make this happen:

Create A Reading Budget – you create a budget for everything else in your life, why not reading? By doing this you'll know how much you have to spend (and when you have it to spend) when you are surfing the Amazon.com and BN.com book web sites.

Get A Library Card – remember the library from your childhood? Good news – it's still there. No matter where you live, no matter how big or how small your local library is, almost all libraries have some sort of inter-library loan program that can provide you with access to just about any book that you might want. Check it out!

Become A Sale Shopper – you don't have to buy the newest books immediately when they come out. Look for the slow seasons and stock up then. Right after Christmas most books stores have great sales so that they can get rid of the extra stock that they bought for the holiday season.

Befriend Local Used Books Stores – when I lived in Dallas there was a bookstore called Books-A-Million that was huge and always seemed to have a book in the area that I was looking for. If you don't have a local used books store then you can always make use of half.com which is Ebay's used book store.

Other Ways To Become An Expert

With all that being said, reading books isn't the ONLY way to become an expert in your selected area (although it is the best way). You can always **supplement your reading** by doing additional things like:

Searching The Internet – however, you need to remember that you can't always trust what you find on the Internet. Verify, verify, verify.

Ask Questions Of Smart People – seek out people who know more about something than you do and take them out to lunch. Ask them questions and then pay attention to what they have to say.

Read The Newspaper – yeah, just like your parents used to do. You just might be amazed at what you find out is going on around you.

Watch DVDs – no, not Hollywood films, but rather instructional ones that will teach you something.

Attend Seminars – since you are trying to become an expert, take the time to go see other experts and learn from them – how did they get their knowledge and how do they use it.

Final Thoughts

One characteristic of an expert that many speakers never realize is that they are **always growing, always changing**. One self-help book that I read awhile back had a great way of putting it. The author suggested that we should plan on reinventing ourselves every year – sorta a you 1.0, followed by a you 2.0.

By doing this you will always have **fresh and interesting things** to tell your audiences about and they will always be interested in hearing what you have to say.

Make the effort to become an expert and you'll be able to intimately connect with your audience and make a **lasting impact** in their lives.

Chapter 4

Speaker Alert: Make Me Laugh — Or Else

Chapter 4: Speaker Alert: Make Me Laugh — Or Else

Stop. How funny was the last speech that you gave? What – you were talking about how best to diversify a 401k basket of investments in order to incorporate more foreign exchange funds & there's nothing funny about that? Wrong. You're not trying hard enough. **Stop being not funny**.

Learn To Be Funny From A Politician

Every speech counts. Especially if you are trying to get elected. If there was any group of speakers who needed to find a way to get people to remember them & their message, it would be **politicians**. They have three goals every time they give a speech:

1. Promote their policies
2. Boost their accomplishments while minimizing their opponents
3. Impress people with their moral upstanding character & leadership skills

Politicians know that **humor is a powerful speaking tool**. They use it to both make a point as well as to illustrate that point for their (or your) audience.

In the end, it's all about getting votes. You're probably not running for anything right now, but **why waste a speech**?

Why Humor Is So Powerful When You Are Speaking

Every speech that you give is your next chance to **change the world**. Adding humor to your speaking style isn't something that you can put off until "sometime", you've got to do it right now.

The reason that humor works so well comes down to **five basic "levers"** that every audience has. Gene Perret who won several Emmys for his work in television has spent a lot of time researching what these levers do to an audience:

Humor Makes You More Likable: I don't care how much of a jerk you are in real life, if you start to work more humor into your speeches your audiences will start to like you better than your family does. Perret points out that it's really hard to laugh with a person if you don't like them – make your audience laugh and they'll love you forever.

Build Credibility Using Humor: Who are you to talk to anyone about anything? Somewhat amazingly, audiences associate the ability to be funny with wisdom. When you can joke with your audience about 401k plans, they'll settle back and say to themselves "gosh, if he can joke about this stuff then he must know it really well". Whether or not you really do know it really doesn't matter anymore after this.

Get Respect Using Humor: Some of the worst speeches that I've ever had to sit through were ones where the speaker was too full of himself / herself. I quickly tuned them out – I don't have time for blowhards. When you kid around with your audience you're telling them "I'm one of you". When they understand that you "get" them, you will have hooked them and they'll pay attention to you for the rest of your speech.

Make People Want To Listen Using Humor: When you say something funny, people laugh. If they're not listening, then they miss out. Nobody likes to miss out on something that's funny. When you work humor into your speeches and people start to laugh, then all of those other people who are busy reading email and sending text messages will start to look around and wonder what they are missing out on. Very quickly those iPhones and Blackberry's will go away and you'll have their attention.

Make People Remember What You Say Using Humor: Stay home if you are going to give a speech that nobody is going to remember. Why bother? What humor does is it creates the possibility that people will remember the joke, and if they do then there's just a chance that they might remember what your point was that you made the joke about.

Final Thoughts

Stop wasting my time. If you want to get up there and give a dry, lifeless speech that has no humor in it then you may as well stay at home and just **send me an email** with your main points.

If, however, you want me to walk away thinking that you know what you are talking about and **remembering what you said**, then that's another story. The only way that that's going to happen is if you start to work some **humor** into your speech. No, you don't have to turn into a stand-up comedian; however, you do need to make me crack a smile or at least chuckle. Get me to do that and you've spent your time well.

Chapter 5

Hey Baby, Come Here Often?

Chapter 5: Hey Baby, Come Here Often?

Just like a cheesy pick-up line, the first words that come out of your mouth when you are giving a speech will determine if you are going to get lucky with this audience. Unlike a wanna-be Casanova in a bar, you (normally) don't have an opportunity to buy your audience a drink, so you're going to have work extra hard to make your opening lines do all the work for you if you want to have any hope of **sweeping the audience off of their feet**. How are you going to score?

The 4 Questions That Every Audience Asks Themselves

Hopefully you've been given a great introduction. Now it's your turn to speak. Dana LaMon who was the Toastmasters' 1982 World Champion of Public-Speaking says that as your audience awaits the start of your speech, they are sitting there asking themselves **four questions**:

1. Am I going to take the time to listen to this speaker?
2. Am I going to benefit from what he / she talks about?
3. Will they say anything that is valuable that I can take and use?
4. Will anything that they say be worthwhile for me to take action on?

If you **waste your first few words**, then I can tell you what the answers to these questions will be – and you're not going to like it!

Am I going to take the time to listen to this speaker?

Aren't those Blackberry's and iPhones just the coolest? Today more than ever your audience has **other things that they can do** while you are talking if they aren't interested in what you have to say. Let's pretend for just a moment that today's jaded audience starts by answering this question with a "No". Now you're not just trying to move them to a "yes", instead you've got the doubly hard job of moving them off of "no" and over to "yes".

Every speech that you give will be different, but you can lose your audience every time if you make one of the following **common speaker mistakes**:

Thanking Anybody: the first words out of your mouth in a speech are the equivalent of waterfront property in real estate – super valuable. Why would you waste them by saying something like "I'd like to thank the Dairy Producers Council for inviting me to talk to you today..."

Calling Out Important People In The Audience: I don't care if Obama himself is sitting in the front row or your audience, wasting your opening words pointing out that you've got important people in the audience is just you complementing yourself and nobody really wants to hear you do that.

A Man Walks Into A Bar...: Why would anyone waste an opening of a speech on an old, tired joke that has nothing to do with what they are going to be talking about? I've seen this happen over and over again. Even when the joke is funny, all too often it doesn't lead anywhere – it was just a cute thing to say and then the speaker starts his / her speech and the opportunity to grab the audience's attention has been lost forever

The Title Of This Speech Is...: What? Why would I be sitting in the audience if I didn't already know what you are going to be talking about? Also, don't waste an opening by introducing yourself "My name is Bob Johnson and I'd like to talk to you about ..." Assume that either the audience already knows this information or they just don't care about it. Get on with the meat of what you are there to talk about

Am I going to benefit from what he / she talks about?

I'm a busy guy and assuming that you have somehow gotten me to answer "yes" to the first question, you sure don't have any guarantee that I'm going to **keep listening to you** – I've got a lot of email that I could be working my way through on my iPhone.

Right off the bat you are going to have to very concisely tell me **why I should care about what you're going to be talking about** for the next 30 minutes or so. Whatever this speech's purpose is, you're going to have to keep it short – one sentence is the rule. If it's longer than that, I'm not going to pay attention. Do this and there is a chance that you're audience will remember what you said after you are done.

Will they say anything that is valuable that I can take and use?

What's the **greatest complement** that a speaker can receive? Is it a standing ovation? Nope. It's when your audience whips out a pencil and starts to take notes.

In every speech there are some "**nuggets**" that you want your audience to remember and use after you are done talking. It's your job as a speaker to make these pieces of actionable information easy for your audience to find and remember. Saying things like "Here are three things that you might want to write down…" are a great way to motivate your audience to take notes.

Will anything that they say be worthwhile for me to take action on?

I've taken notes at a lot of speeches that I've attended and then I've gone home and **filed them away** somewhere and that was the end of the story. As a speaker this is exactly what you don't want to have happen.

Instead, you want the information that you are passing on to be used – you really want to **change people's lives**. To get your audience to take action you need to do three things: you need to tell them what you want them to do, you need to tell them why they should do it, and then you need to tell them that they can be successful in doing it.

What All Of This Means For You

When I'm coaching speakers who are struggling to break through to the next level in their speaking skills, we spend a lot of time working on the opening of their speech **because it is so important**. There are an almost unlimited number of ways that you can successfully grab an audience's attention with your first few words. Unfortunately, there is an almost equal number of ways that you can lose them forever.

You'll lose them if you spend your time thinking about yourself when you are putting your speech together. If, instead, you spend your time putting yourself **in the position of your audience** and making sure that you answer the questions that are running though their minds, then you'll find the words that will grab their imagination from the get-go and you'll be off and running with the best speech of your life.

Chapter 6

Don't Toast The Holidays: How Presenters Can Give A Toast Without Toasting A Relationship

Chapter 6: Don't Toast The Holidays: How Presenters Can Give A Toast Without Toasting A Relationship

It's the holiday season once again, a virtual minefield of social speaking opportunities. I can just see it now: you're at the office Christmas party, there will probably be some sort of food served, drinks will flow, and then someone will do it – they'll stand up and give a toast. Oh, oh – now it's your turn to do the same thing. How are you going to do this without looking like a fool or destroying your relationship with the person(s) of honor (your boss perhaps?)

First off, get rid of any plans that you might have to say something naughty. Rarely this might go over well; however, more often than not it falls flat on its face and so just say "no". Michael Varma is a professional speaker who has seen his fair share of toasting disasters and he's got some advice for all of us.

Michael says that when you are giving a toast, you should always start out by introducing yourself – in a crowd of people, there are probably a bunch of folks who don't know who you are. Also spell out how you are related to the person(s) of honor because this will help to make your toast clearer. Michael suggests that your actual toast have three characteristics: make it brief, make it bold, and then be done with it.

A toast is NOT a speech! Mark Twain probably said it best when he recommended that toasts should never be longer than 1 minute. The longer your toast, the less impact that it will have. The "air time" that you are taking for your toast belongs to everyone and you need to use as little of it as possible.

When you are giving a toast, this is not the time to be shy. You are probably talking to a noisy room in which people may be eating, drinking, and having their own side conversations. You need to speak up! Your goal should be to speak loudly enough that everyone in the room, including the folks in the back, can hear you clearly.

When you are done speaking, shut up and sit down. Yes you've just given a performance; however, this event is not all about you so don't do any bowing or waving. Shut your mouth and sit down so that everyone can once again return their attention to the person(s) of honor.

If you want your toast to be memorable, then the trick is to tell a story. I must once again reemphasize a key point – keep it clean! You shouldn't tell stories about old girlfriends at a wedding and you shouldn't tell stories about stealing office supplies at the annual Christmas party. Instead, tell a story that shows the person(s) of honor in a good light. Oh, and keep it to under a minute.

My recommendation is to get a little sappy, a little funny, and hopefully that will be just right for a toast at any holiday gathering.

Chapter 7

What's More Important: What You Say Or Who Is Saying It?

Chapter 7: What's More Important: What You Say Or Who Is Saying It?

So here's a question for you to ponder: what is more important – the words that you say or how you say them? This is one of the classic questions that gets asked about public speaking. Could you pick up a fantastically written speech and deliver it in a way that would create the same (or better) reaction in the audience that the original presenter got?

It's All About Teamwork

In the end, it turns out that this is really a **trick question**. The answer is that you can't have one without the other. It's the combination of both the material and the speaker who presents the material that causes the desired reaction in the audience.

One thing that too many speakers don't take the time to realize is that each speech needs to be tailored to meet the **unique needs** of the speaker who is delivering it. You have your own unique style (you are loud, you are quiet, etc.) and nobody else presents a speech the same way that you do.

The one thing that we need to be careful to not do is to try to present someone else's speech. Trying to deliver a speech that was created for someone else will be just like trying to wear clothes that were **custom tailored** for somebody else's dimensions. It just won't look good.

How To Match Your Next Speech To Your Speaking Style

If you can accept the idea that it takes both a good speaker and a good speech to deliver a winning presentation, then the next obvious question is **how can you do this successfully?**

Gene Perret spent his career writing television shows and comedy material. He knows a thing or two about tailoring the material to the presenter. He has **three suggestions** on what you need to do in order to ensure that your next speech connects with your audience in a powerful way:

Be True To Your Speech: A speaker who is talking about a subject that he/she either doesn't believe in or doesn't care about will never be able to connect with the audience. I don't care how great of an actor you think that you are, if you don't believe in what you are saying then it will eventually show through to your audience and they will dismiss your message. If you don't believe me, then think back to some of those corporate speeches that we've all seen when executive management tries to convince the staff that everything is ok and that there's nothing to worry about. That message never flies!

Match Your Words To Your Style: I have a friend who is a very flamboyant speaker – he's all over the stage and his arms are always waving in the air. Once upon a time I happened to see him deliver a very somber speech about a sad set of circumstances that had caused a business to fail. The speech went over like a lead balloon. My friend's normal speaking style had to be greatly restricted because of the speech's subject matter and so the audience got conflicting messages – they saw a lot of bottled up energy, but were hearing and seeing a very low energy speech. Don't make this mistake – when you give a speech, make sure that the material that you are presenting matches your style of speaking.

Stay Competent: we all have areas of knowledge that we are strong in. Either we've spent the time studying in order to understand this area or we've worked in a related field. That being said, there will be occasions that we'll be asked to talk on a topic that we know nothing about. Don't do it! We all do certain things well, and a bunch of other things not so well. If you end up talking about a topic that you don't know well, then all of your weak points will show up during your speech and you won't be able to connect with your audience.

What All Of This Means For You

A speaker by themselves or a speech by itself has very little value. It's only when the two are brought together that **the real magic** of an effective presentation can happen. As speakers, we need to understand that we have our own unique style and we need to make sure that we never try to present a speech that has been created for someone else because it just won't work.

In order to harness both **the power** of a speech and our personal style, we need to make sure that we believe in what we are saying, matching our speaking style, and only talk about topics that we know something about.

Combined with the right speech we can **move audiences**. Now all we need to do in order to make sure that our next speech is the perfect combination of words and style is to practice, practice, practice…!

Chapter 8

Get It Done: Thinking On Your Feet And Building A Speech Real Quick

Chapter 8: Get It Done: Thinking On Your Feet And Building A Speech Real Quick

If I asked you to give a speech, how much time would you need to get ready to give the speech (including writing it)? Could you do it if I gave you half as much time? **How about if I gave you 5 minutes?** We don't always control the situations in which we are asked to give a speech, knowing how to prepare one in just a few minutes is a key speaker skill...

Just Where Do You Start?

I guess the best place to start our discussion about what to do when you are put on the spot and asked to deliver a speech **RIGHT NOW**, is at the beginning. It's pretty clear that if somebody is asking you to give a speech all of sudden, then they can't be too picky about what you'll talk about.

This is where you get some latitude. In order to pull off this quick speech creation thing, **you're going to have to pick a topic to speak about that you already both know and love**. I'm hoping that it's clear to you that you still need to keep your audience in mind, but because of the short amount of time that you have, this is the one time that you get to start with yourself first.

Since it is so critical that you already know your topic well, pick what you want to speak about and then spend a moment or two trying to think about **how you can make this subject appeal to your audience**. For example, if what you know really well is how to schedule family vacations and you're going to be talking to a group of mothers, then focusing on the logistics of what to pack and keeping the family happy during the trip will generally be what you need to focus on in order to make your story appeal to them.

It's All In The Details

Although you won't have a lot of time to create your on-the-spot speech, **it still needs to be interesting**. A lack of time to prepare a speech is not a license to be boring. It's time to whip out a piece of paper, you've got some writing to do.

What you need to write down is **a list of things that you will want to cover in your speech**. This is an important list because it holds the key to making your speech interesting to your audience. Write down the sequence of items that you want to cover, then take a second look at it.

The key here will be to make sure that the material that you will be covering flows. It needs to start some place and then build up to a natural conclusion. If you aren't careful, then due to your limited time it will just be a jumbled collection of pieces of information. Use just a bit of your limited time to sort and rearrange your discussion points so that they present **a complete story**.

Houston, We Have Lift-Off

With picking a topic and creating a list of items to discuss, you will have used up a sizable chunk of the limited time that you have before you'll be on the stage. What to do with the few remaining minutes that you have left? Simple: **rehearse**.

As we all know, the first few words out of your mouth during any speech are the most important – this is how the audience makes their decision whether or not to bother listening to you. You've got to mentally practice what you are going to say. Try out different phrases and word orders until you come up with something **that works best for you**.

What All Of This Means For You

Sorry, you don't run the world just yet. This means that no matter how good of a planner you are, there will be times in which you get surprised by a request to give a speech **with little or no time for you to prepare what you are going to say**.

See this challenge as an opportunity to **grow your speaking skills**. Pick a topic to speak on that you already know well. Shape it to meet the interests of your audience. Make sure that you take a moment or two to rehearse what you are going to say in your head so that your first words will resonate with your audience.

In the end, if you believe in yourself and your ability to deliver a great speech, **you will do just fine**. In fact, who knows, maybe you are one of those speakers who gives the best speech of their life when they have had the least amount of time to prepare for it!

Chapter 9

You Are A Superhero Speaker: You've Got Word Power!

Chapter 9: You Are A Superhero Speaker: You've Got Word Power!

As speakers we have a tendency to focus on the things that scare us the most – forgetting our words, nervous body tics, etc. and we can often overlook the things that really count: making an impression on our audience. We see these images of sharply dressed orators presenting fantastic multimedia presentations and we sigh to ourselves and say "I could never do that". Well it turns out that you don't have to. You can be **a powerfully effective speaker** who is sought after by many just by taking the time to carefully pick the words that you use.

Why Do Words Have So Much Power

I don't know about you, but when I know that I have a speech to give, **I hurry to get the speech written** so that I can start to practice it. Hopefully I've got a reasonably clear idea in my head of what I want to say and I rush to get it down on paper (ok, so I type it into a computer) before I forget what point I want to make. If I'm nervous about the audience that I'll be addressing, then I'll take some time and worry about the "flow" of the speech, but in all honesty that's pretty much it.

Clearly I'm skipping the most important point: **it's all about the words that we use**. Sure, the structure of the speech is important also just like the design of a house is important; however, it's what you build the house out of that is just as (if not more) critical. Words have power.

Just think about **the most powerful speeches that we've all heard**: "Ask not what your country can do for you, but what you can do for your country" and "I have a dream...". I don't think that these words were in the first draft of either of these speeches, rather the authors went back and spent the time to get their words right. The fact that all of these years later we can still recall them shows that they were successful.

Words Are Like The Paints You Use To Make A Picture

When we give a speech, the big question is what are we really trying to do? We want to have our audience share an experience with us. We want them to **feel and see what we feel and see**. They don't have to agree with us, but we want them to understand how we see a given situation. If we're sad, we want them to experience sadness. If we're happy, then we want to feel our happiness.

As a speaker, at the end of the day all that we have to work with to accomplish this goal of connecting with our audiences **are words**. What words allow us to do is to paint a picture in the minds of our audience. I like to think of choosing the right words as being the same thing as an artist choosing the right colors with which to create a painting.

If I gave you just a three colors, red, green, and blue, **could you create a painting?** Yes, in fact you could combine these three colors to make many more colors and if you had some artistic ability you could probably create a very nice painting. However, something would be missing. If we stepped back once you were done and looked at your creation I think that we'd both agree that you'd captured the essence of whatever you were painting; however, something would be missing – depth.

If instead of restricting you to just using three colors I let you use every color in the world, just imagine what you could create now! The final product would be **much richer** – you would have been able to capture both depth and subtlety that was not possible when you had just three colors to work with.

All of the same things can be said about using words in a speech. If you keep it simple and only use plain, everyday words then your speech **will be flat and lack depth**. Sure you can do it this way, but who's going to want to listen to that?

If instead you take the time to carefully pick and hone your words so that you use just the right word in just the right spot, then you will have made a speech that **allows you to connect with your audience**. When you are done, your audience will have a mental image that they can take home and treasure forever.

What All Of This Means For You

The most powerful tool that a speaker has are **the words that make up the speech** that he / she is giving. Just racing to throw a speech together and not spending any time to craft the words that you will use means that you are missing out on one of your most powerful speaking tools.

Words are how we **connect with our audience**. In order to make a lasting impression on an audience we need to use the right words that will allow us to create a vivid mental image in every member of our audience's head.

It doesn't take that much of an extra effort to make our words work for us. Reviewing your next speech and asking yourself if the words that you are using will allow you to connect with your audience will tell you where you stand. If your words aren't painting a powerful image for you, then **get some more colors to paint with!**

Chapter 10

The Best Speeches Have A Lot Of You In Them

Chapter 10: The Best Speeches Have A Lot Of You In Them

Congratulations – you've been asked to give a speech. **Got one to give?** Unless someone has asked you to deliver a speech that you've already given multiple times, you're probably in the spot that most speakers find themselves all too often – standing in the middle of tracks while the train known as your speaking date comes racing towards you. What's an accidental communicator to do?

What Makes A Speech Memorable

Let's all agree on one thing first: if your speech is not memorable, then **it's really not worth giving**. Starting from that point, you may start to feel some pressure – how the heck are you going to make your next speech memorable?

It turns out that there are a lot of ways to do this; however, the simplest way to do it is to **work more of "you" into your speech**. This means that you've got to find ways to share just exactly what makes you you with your audience. This boils down to one thing: you need to tell your audience some of your stories.

As I think back over all of the speeches that I've had an opportunity to listen to over my life, the handful that really stand out are the ones in which the speaker **did a good job of sharing**. You've got to remember that before they opened their mouth, I didn't know anything about them. However, the personal stories that they told were so engrossing that they hooked me – I not only listened, but I've remembered their stories over the years since they spoke.

How To Go About Uncovering Your Stories

Fantastic you say, **but I don't have any stories to tell**. Or at least no stories that anyone is going to want to hear. I hear you there – once upon a time I thought the same thing.

It turns out that **your life story is a great story** that, told well, everyone will want to hear. Now, you've been asked to give a speech and no, they haven't really asked you to come and spend the time talking about yourself. However, adding your personal stories to the speech will make any speech have more impact.

One of the reasons that incorporating your personal stories into a speech can lend so much impact to what you are saying is because **you were there** – you actually lived what you are talking about. This means that when you explain what happened, you will describe it using words that will build a vivid mental image for your audience.

Additionally, as you tell your story your body language will naturally **synch with your words**. This means that your audience will be getting a reinforcing message from your body even as you speak.

What All Of This Means To You

All too often when we get asked to deliver a speech we focus on doing the research needed to create a good speech but we neglect to do what it takes to **make a great speech**. A great speech is one that includes more of our personal content in it.

In order to **personalize a story**, we need to include more of our own stories. This means that we need to spend some time thinking about the things that have happened in our lives that would support the topic that we'll be speaking on.

Speakers who can work their personal stories into a speech are the ones that will make a **lasting impact**. As long as you are going to go to the effort of giving a speech, doesn't this seem like a good thing to do?

Chapter 11

What Could Chris Matthews Teach You About Speaking In Public?

Chapter 11: What Could Chris Matthews Teach You About Speaking In Public?

If you've ever wished that there was **a formula** for giving the perfect speech, are you in luck! Chris Matthews is the host of a couple of TV shows including Hardball with Chris Matthews. He gets paid handsomely for the work that he does now, but he got his start as a humble political speechwriter. Based on all of that experience, he's come up with a way to give the perfect speech...

It's All In His Book

Chris has written a book called Life's a Campaign: What Politics Has Taught Me About Friendship, Rivalry, Reputation, and Success. In this book he lays out his **six-step program** for creating the perfect speech.

Step #1: Break The Ice – When you first take the stage, nobody knows who you are. The first thing that you need to do is to put your audience at ease. One of the best ways to do this is to make a small joke that is based on current events: the room is too cold, it's raining outside, the local sports team just won / lost. Whatever you say the purpose is to relax your audience and let them know that you are one of them.

Step #2: Show Some Skin – Everyone in the audience didn't just show up there by accident. They are there for a reason – they want to hear what you are going to talk about. Give them a quick "tweet" about what you'll be talking about just to capture their attention.

Step #3 – Share A Story: You need to be able to explain why YOU are up there on the stage. Tell the audience the story of how you were approached and asked to present. The purpose of telling this story is to get your audience to both settle down for your main speech while at the same time building excitement for what comes next.

Step #4 – Let Them Have It With Both Barrels – Now is the time to give your audience what they came for: your & message and your content. You may be delivering a lot of information so be sure to break it up into bite sized pieces.

Step #5 – Lighten Up: you've got to communicate to your audience that the real meat of your speech is now down. The best way to do this is to tell another story, but this time keep it light and make it fun.

Step #6 – Launch Them: At the very end of your speech you want to get your audience excited about what they've learned from you. Revisit the reason that you were asked to speak and make sure that you leave them with clear direction on how they can use the information that you've given them.

What All Of This Means For You

Ok, so I wasn't completely honest with you – there's **no magic formula** that will work for every speech. However, Chris Matthews does have a pretty good approach.

Taking the time to **initially connect with your audience**, telling stories, and then sharing the content that your audience desires is a powerful way to get your message across.

Chris' technique should give you **a place to start** the next time you have to create a speech. Use these six steps to giving a speech in order to truly connect with your audience.

Chapter 12

---

4 Things That You Should Never Talk About

Chapter 12: 4 Things That You Should Never Talk About

The next time that you are given an opportunity to create and deliver a speech, do me a favor and stop, put your pencil done before you start to write. I can just imagine what's running through your mind: the magic words that will come spilling out of your mouth and will entertain and entrance your audience. Umm, unless of course they don't. If you **talk about the wrong things**, then your speech will go nowhere quickly. Maybe we should have a chat about what you shouldn't be talking about...

The Big Three

In every speaker's life, hopefully there is someone who takes them aside early on and tells them the three topics that are absolutely off limits: **race, religion, and sexuality**. Yeah, yeah – if you are talking on one of these topics, then it's ok, but if you're not, then you need to stay far, far away.

The reason for this is because each of these topics are **polarizing flash points** that will instantly divide your audience. Some will agree with what you say, some won't and you will have lost your audience.

Too Much Personal Info

As long as we are talking about things that you shouldn't be talking about, let's make sure that you know that sharing is good, **but too much sharing is bad**. I'm not even talking about the embarrassing personal stuff, instead I'm talking about the boring details of each of our lives.

I'm sure that we all have hobbies and personality quirks that we may find interesting or endearing. However, they aren't. This is why you always want to **test your speeches with friends who will be honest with you**. If that personal story just isn't doing it, then it needs to go away before you hurt an audience with it.

Personal Success Stories

So you saved a busload of schoolchildren from a pack of rampaging wild elephants. Yawn. Look, if you've done something impressive, that's pretty cool. However, do you really think that you can tell me about it **without coming across as someone who is bragging?**

It takes a very careful skill for a speaker to share a story of personal success with an audience in the right way. **You have to have a reason for telling the story**. That reason has to have something to do with your audience. You had better be telling them how they can have the same type of success that you had or the story will just end up making your audience feel inadequate.

Book Reports

Any time that we have a speech to give that includes **describing a sequence of events**, such as a trip that we took, how something is manufactured, etc., we run the risk of delivering a book report that nobody wants to hear. You would be amazed at how many times I've had to sit though speeches that started out with "I'd now like to tell you about the 17 steps that we had to go through to solve this problem."

Even if something took 17 steps to do, you don't have to cover them all in your speech. Take some mercy on your audience and **trim it down to two or three steps** and tell them to talk to you to get more details if they want them. You must always think about how your speech is going to sound to your audience before you deliver it.

Bad Objects

I like **a visual aid** just as much as the next speaker, but sometimes they can work against you. Depending on the size of your room, a visual aid can be either too big and overshadow you or too small and not visible to your audience.

Keep in mind that **you are the star of your speech** – nothing else is. This means that if you choose to use something else that will allow your audience to take their eyes off of you, then it had better be the right object for the right audience.

What All Of This Means For You

As speakers we like to focus on what we can include in our next speech. However, it might be just as important to spend some time **worrying about what we should not be putting into that speech**.

The **obvious topics** that shouldn't be included include race, religion, and sexuality. However, boring personal habits, overblown success stories, book reports, and poorly selected visual aids can also bring your next speech down.

The key to avoiding including things that will take away from your message is to **put yourself in the place of your audience**. If you can create a speech that has only good content and no bad content, then you will have created a speech that everyone is going to want to hear.

It's from the forge of failure that the steel of success is formed.

Hard Work Does Not Guarantee Success, But Success Does Not Happen Without Hard Work.

\- Dr. Jim Anderson

Create Speeches That Motivate Your Audiences And Get Your Message Heard!

Dr. Jim Anderson is available to provide training and coaching on the topics that are the most important to people who have to speak in public: how can I create a speech that people want to hear and how can I deliver in a way that will allow me to connect with my audience and get my point across to them?

Dr. Anderson believes that in order to both learn and remember what he says, speakers need to laugh. Each one of his speeches is full of fun and humor so that what he says "sticks" with everyone.

Dr. Anderson's Public Speaking Training Includes:

1. How to plan your next speech: pick your purpose and understand your audience.
2. What's the best way to get PowerPoint and Keynote to work with you, not against you?
3. What do you need to do when you are presenting in order to truly connect with your audience?

Dr. Jim Anderson presents over 100 speeches per year. To invite Dr. Anderson to speak at your event, contact him at:

Phone: 813-418-6970 or
Email: jim@BlueElephantConsulting.com

Blue Elephant Consulting

Speaking. Negotiating. Managing. Marketing.

64

Photo Credits:

Cover - ashley.adcox

https://www.flickr.com/photos/viggum/

Chapter 1 - Travis Wise

https://www.flickr.com/photos/photographingtravis/

Chapter 2 - Alan Levine

https://www.flickr.com/photos/cogdog/

Chapter 3 - Michael Li

https://www.flickr.com/photos/han_shot_first/

Chapter 4 - Marc Kjerland

https://www.flickr.com/photos/marckjerland/

Chapter 5 - Todd X.

https://www.flickr.com/photos/toddx/

Chapter 6 - Sheep purple

https://www.flickr.com/photos/sheeppurple/

Chapter 7 – Wikipedia

https://en.wikipedia.org/wiki/Winston_Churchill

Chapter 8 – Julian Lim

https://www.flickr.com/photos/julianlim/

Chapter 9 - Nina A.J.

https://www.flickr.com/photos/nicasaurusrex/

Chapter 10 - Dominik Gubi

https://www.flickr.com/photos/nacaseven/

Chapter 11 - Chetly Zarko

https://www.flickr.com/photos/chetly/

Chapter 12 - Brandon Anderson

https://www.flickr.com/photos/nullvalue/

Other Books By
The Author

Product Management

- How Product Managers Can Sell More Of Their Product: Tips & Techniques For Product Managers To Better Understand How To Sell Their Product

- How Product Managers Can Sell More Of Their Product: Tips & Techniques For Product Managers To Better Understand How To Sell Their Product

- How To Create A Successful Product That Customers Will Want: Techniques For Product Managers To Boost Product Sales And Increase Customer Satisfaction

- What Product Managers Need To Know About World-Class Product Development: How Product Managers Can Create Successful Products

- How Product Managers Can Learn To Understand Their Customers: Techniques For Product Managers To Better Understand What Their Customers Really Want

- Product Management Secrets: Techniques For Product Managers To Boost Produ Michael Kct Sales And Increase Customer Satisfaction

- Product Development Lessons For Product Managers: How Product Managers Can Create Successful Products

- Customer Lessons For Product Managers: Techniques For Product Managers To Better Understand What Their Customers Really Want

- Product Failure Lessons For Product Managers: Examples Of Products That Have Failed For Product Managers To Learn From

- Communication Skills For Product Managers: The Communication Skills That Product Managers Need To Know How To Use In Order To Have A Successful Product

- How To Have A Successful Product Manager Career: The Things That You Need To Be Doing TODAY In Order To Have A Successful Product Manager Career

- Product Manager Product Success: How to keep your product on track and make it become a success

Public Speaking

- How To Organize A Speech In Order To Make Your Point: How to put together a speech that will capture and hold your audience's attention

- Changing How You Speak To Overcome Your Fear Of Speaking: Change techniques that will transform a speech into a memorable event

- Delivering Excellence: How To Give Presentations That Make A Difference: Presentation techniques that will transform a speech into a memorable event

- Tools Speakers Need In Order To Give The Perfect Speech: What tools to use to create your next speech so that your message will be remembered forever!

- How To Create A Speech That Will Be Remembered

- Secrets To Organizing A Speech For Maximum Impact: How to put together a speech that will capture and hold your audience's attention

- How To Become A Better Speaker By Changing How You Speak: Change techniques that will transform a speech into a memorable event

- How To Give A Great Presentation: Presentation techniques that will transform a speech into a memorable event

- How To Rehearse In Order To Give The Perfect Speech: How to effectively rehearse your next speech to that your message be remembered forever!

- Secrets To Creating The Perfect Speech: How to create a speech that will make your message be remembered forever!

- Secrets To Organizing The Perfect Speech: How to organize the best speech of your life!

- Secrets To Planning The Perfect Speech: How to plan to give the best speech of your life

- How To Show What You Mean During A Presentation: How to use visual techniques to transform a speech into a memorable event

CIO Skills

- New IT Technology Issues Facing CIOs: How CIOs Can Stay On Top Of The Changes In The Technology That Powers The Company

- Keeping The Barbarians Out: How CIOs Can Secure Their Department and Company: Tips And Techniques For CIOs To Use In Order To Secure Both Their IT Department And Their Company

- What CIOs Need To Know In Order To Successfully Manage An IT Department: Decision Making Skills That Every CIO Needs To Have In Order To Be Able To Make The Right Choices

- Becoming A Powerful And Effective Leader: Tips And Techniques That IT Managers Can Use In Order To Develop Leadership Skills

- CIO Secrets For Growing Innovation: Tips And Techniques For CIOs To Use In Order To Make Innovation Happen In Their IT Department

- Your Success As A CIO Depends On How Well You Communicate: Tips And Techniques For CIOs To Use In Order To Become Better Communicators

- What CIOs Need To Know About Working With Partners: Techniques For CIOs To Use In Order To Be Able To Successfully Work With Partners

- Critical CIO Management Skills: Decision Making Skills That Every CIO Needs To Have In Order To Be Able To Make The Right Choices

- How CIOs Can Make Innovation Happen: Tips And Techniques For CIOs To Use In Order To Make Innovation Happen In Their IT Department

- CIO Communication Skills Secrets: Tips And Techniques For CIOs To Use In Order To Become

Better Communicators

- Managing Your CIO Career: Steps That CIOs Have To Take In Order To Have A Long And Successful Career

- CIO Business Skills: How CIOs can work effectively with the rest of the company!

IT Manager Skills

- How IT Managers Can Use New Technology To Meet Today's IT Challenges: Technologies That IT Managers Can Use In Order to Make Their Teams More Productive

- How To Build High Performance IT Teams: Tips And Techniques That IT Managers Can Use In Order To Develop Productive Teams

- Save Yourself, Save Your Job – How To Manage Your IT Career: Secrets That IT Managers Can Use In Order To Have A Successful Career

- Growing Your CIO Career: How CIOs Can Work With The Entire Company In Order To Be Successful

- How IT Managers Can Make Innovation Happen: Tips And Techniques For IT Managers To Use In Order To Make Innovation Happen In Their Teams

- Staffing Skills IT Managers Must Have: Tips And Techniques That IT Managers Can Use In Order To Correctly Staff Their Teams

- Secrets Of Effective Leadership For IT Managers: Tips And Techniques That IT Managers Can Use In Order To Develop Leadership Skills

- IT Manager Career Secrets: Tips And Techniques That IT Managers Can Use In Order To Have A Successful Career

- IT Manager Budgeting Skills: How IT Managers Can Request, Manage, Use, And Track Their Funding

- Secrets Of Managing Budgets: What IT Managers Need To Know In Order To Understand How Their Company Uses Money

Negotiating

- Getting What You Want In A Negotiation By Learning How To Signal: How To Develop The Skill Of Effective Signaling In A Negotiation In Order To Get The Best Possible Outcome

- Exploring How To Get The Deal That You Want In A Negotiation: How To Develop The Skill Of Exploring What Is Possible In A Negotiation In Order To Reach The Best Possible Deal

- Use The Power Of Arguing To Win Your Next Negotiation: How To Develop The Skill Of Effective Arguing In A Negotiation In Order To Get The Best Possible Outcome

- Learn How To Signal In Your Next Negotiation: How To Develop The Skill Of Effective Signaling In A Negotiation In Order To Get The Best Possible Outcome

- Learn The Skill Of Exploring In A Negotiation: How To Develop The Skill Of Exploring What Is Possible In A Negotiation In Order To Reach The Best Possible Deal

- Learn How To Argue In Your Next Negotiation: How To Develop The Skill Of Effective Arguing In A Negotiation In Order To Get The Best Possible Outcome|

- How To Open Your Next Negotiation: How To Start A Negotiation In Order To Get The Best Possible Outcome

- Preparing For Your Next Negotiation: What You Need To Do BEFORE A Negotiation Starts In Order To Get The Best Possible Deal

- Learn How To Package Trades In Your Next Negotiation

- All Good Things Come To An End: How To Close A Negotiation - How To Develop The Skill Of Closing In Order To Get The Best Possible Outcome From A Negotiation

- Take No Prisoners In Your Next Negotiation: How To Start A Negotiation In Order To Get The Best Possible Outcome

Miscellaneous

- How To Heal A Broken Leg – Fast!: Understanding how to deal with a broken leg in order to start walking again quickly

- How Software Defined Networking (SDN) Is Going To Change Your World Forever: The Revolution In Network Design And How It Affects You

- The Power Of Virtualization: How It Affects Memory, Servers, and Storage: The Revolution In Creating Virtual Devices And How It Affects You

- The Internet-Enabled Successful School District Superintendent: How To Use The Internet To Boost Parental Involvement In Your Schools

- Power Distribution Unit (PDU) Secrets: What Everyone Who Works In A Data Center Needs To Know!

- Making The Jump: How To Land Your Dream Job When You Get Out Of College!

How To Use The Internet To Create Successful Students And Involved Parents

"How to create a speech that will make your message be remembered forever!"

This book has been written with one goal in mind – to show you how you can create a great speech. We're going to show you what you need to do in order to make your next speech both persuasive and remembered!

Let's Make Your Next Speech A Success!

What You'll Find Inside:

- **SIZE MATTERS – SHAPING YOUR SPEECH TO MATCH YOUR AUDIENCE**

- **THE SECRET TO BECOMING AN EXPERT IN ANYTHING**

- **GET IT DONE: THINKING ON YOUR FEET AND BUILDING A SPEECH REAL QUICK**

- **4 THINGS THAT YOU SHOULD NEVER TALK ABOUT**

Dr. Jim Anderson brings his 25 years of real-world experience to this book. He's delivered speeches at some of the world's largest firms as well as at many conferences. He's going to show you what you need to do in order to make your next speech a success!